650 | Summer Jobs

Edited by Edward McCann

650 | WHERE WRITERS READ
Founder / Editor • Edward McCann
Executive Producer • Richard Kollath
Literary Ombudsman • Steven Lewis
Director of Operations • Jane Kaupp
Design Director • Diane Fokas
Director of Photography • Kevin O'Connor
Chief Audio Engineer • Jesse Chason
Videography / Photography • Sara Caldwell
Copy Editor • Kathleen Stanley
Copy Editor • Shelley Sadler Kenney
Technical Advisor • Conrad Trautmann
Technical Advisor • Stephen Kaupp

Production Assistants
Robert Dennison, Lynn Dennison, Mackenzie Meeks,
Jackie Mercurio, Brian Reagher, and Isabella Fokas

Editorial Committee
Rachel Aydt, Laura Shaine Cunningham, Angela Davis-Gardner,
Karen Dukess, Joseph Goodrich, David Masello, Honor Molloy,
Irene O'Garden, John Pielmeier, Angela Derecas Taylor,
Julie Trelstad, and Gretchen Reed

For Mary Hines McGehee,
with memories of smocks and nametags.

ABOUT 650

Do you remember your first summer job? Of course you do. Whether an exercise in character building or simply a means to an end (and some cash for the weekend), summer jobs have the unique feature of an end date—autumn—creating seasonal brackets around an employment experience that, for many of us, offered entrée into a new realm of young adulthood.

650 is a celebration of writing and the spoken word, a literary forum for personal stories performed five minutes—and 650 words—at a time. Our events at theaters, colleges, and libraries around the country are organized around single, broad topics that invite a range of expression, and recorded performances are added to a digital archive of writers reading their work aloud. The writers and their work receive additional exposure through podcasts, broadcasts, our YouTube channel, and in these printed volumes. The volume you hold in your hands is a collection of stories featured at our very first event at City Winery in New York City.

650 features graduate students and grandparents, first-timers and bestsellers. It's all about the writing, with an emphasis on craft. It's about the choice of one word over another, about the shape of sentences and paragraphs, the arc of a narrative, the poetry of a unique literary voice. If you love language and enjoy a good story, you've come to the right place. To submit your work or attend our shows, visit our website or Facebook page, and join our mailing list.

Please tell your friends about 650, and spread the word about the spoken word.

Ed McCann

Edward McCann, Founder / Editor

READ650.COM
FACEBOOK.COM/READ650

CONTENTS

650 | Summer Jobs

Edited by Edward McCann

ANNABEL MONAGHAN

Annabel Monaghan is the author of two novels for young adults, *A Girl Named Digit* and *Double Digit,* both from Houghton Mifflin Harcourt. She's also the author of *Does This Volvo Make My Butt Look Big?* That essay collection from Fischer Press is based on her column that appears on the *Huffington Post, The Week* and *The Rye Record.* Annabel teaches novel writing at The Writing Institute at Sarah Lawrence College and lives in Rye, New York with her husband and three sons.

MY KID GOT A JOB!

Annabel Monaghan

Raising kids isn't cheap. At first it's just the basics like shelter, clothing, and food, but it quickly spirals out of control into music classes, their own seat on an airplane, and many, many pairs of subtly different cleats. The first time I saw the price of six weeks of summer camp, I gasped and (briefly) considered hanging out with them myself.

Then there's a point when teens need actual cash. Their social lives no longer happen on the playground. They meet up with their friends at and around places that sell pizza and snacks, and without a few bucks it's technically considered loitering. They don't need a lot, but it is at this stage that a parent starts to feel like there's a hole in her pocket.

Which brings me to my big news: My kid got a job. Like for money. I'm trying to let this inevitable but totally unanticipated event sink in. At the most basic level, I'm blown away that he's going to be spending the day doing something that I'm not paying for. It's like he's going to free daycare and coming home with a pocket full of minimum wage.

The best part—while he's at this place (for free, plus salary), he's actually going to learn what $20 means. He already knows what it buys: eight slices of pizza, a trip to the movies, or the price of the basketball he just lost. Frequently it's just one slice of pizza, the change from which gets crumbled in his pocket only to be found and kept by me on laundry day. Any which way, a twenty goes pretty fast.

What he doesn't yet understand is where that $20 comes from. A person with a job quickly learns that a trip to the movies costs nearly three hours of work. Specifically, he's going to have to fetch beach chairs and umbrellas in the hot sun for three hours in order to go to one air-conditioned movie with popcorn. This watershed learning experience marks the exact moment when people get a little pickier about the movies they see.

The $20 lesson is one of the many, many things that you can't teach your kids through talking. I tell them about pre-tax dollars and social security contributions and they give me that look I give people when they talk about grandchildren. I get the concept, but how is this ever going to apply to me? Only the experience of gazing at that first paycheck and thinking, "Wait. That's it?" can teach you what $20 really is.

My mom didn't have a hole in her pocket, so I got my first summer job at fourteen. In 1984, we weren't bound by things like working papers or the truth. I walked into a local store and asked if they were hiring for the summer. When asked my age, I replied,

"How old do I have to be to get the job?" I thought it was a fair enough question. In this way I worked through high school summers folding sweaters, then scooping ice cream, and eventually answering phones. These are all skills that I brought with me into adulthood.

It was the office jobs, filing stuff, that made me really think about the future. Cooped up under the fluorescent lights, breathing the re-circulated air, and watching the clock move backward, I realized that money isn't easy to get. I started to understand how much of someone's life is spent working and the importance of finding a job you enjoy. I had no idea what I wanted to do with my life, but I knew it wasn't putting other people's paper in alphabetical order.

It's ironic how much time and money I spend giving my kids experiences when the best ones are those that they go out and get themselves. And the best part? They're going to feed him lunch.

JACK O'CONNELL

Jack O'Connell is a New York City native presently living on Long Island with his wife, Margaret. He is a working actor with extensive film credits including *Doubt, Big Night, Inside Llewyn Davis, The Paper, God's Pocket, The Quitter, Brazzaville Teenager, Everyday People, The Yards,* and others. Numerous TV credits include *Mad Men, Nurse Jackie,* and *Vinyl,* and Jack is currently seen on the Netflix hit *The Marvelous Mrs. Maisel,* playing Jerry the elevator operator. Jack is a member of Artists Without Walls.

DOCTOR'S ORDERS

Jack O'Connell

"Don't worry Mr. O'Connell. Your insurance covers it." That line alone told me the cardiac rehab service was overpriced. It was late winter, 2001, I was mending from heart by-pass surgery and shopping for a prescribed exercise rehab facility. I was told about measured walks around a track at this state-of-the-art facility. And walking was something I loved to do and the distance prescribed was not a factor. But yes, it was overpriced. I figured I could do this on my own.

A walk around the West End of Jones Beach was three miles. While measuring the distance the next day I came upon a notice, "Seasonal Help Wanted," part-time laborer at $6.91 per hour. I was hired and told the starting date would be mid-April. On April 16, my boss Quinnie handed me a hat, gloves, and a pick stick and told me to go out and collect anything that didn't grow. Along the Bay, past the Coast Guard Station beside the inlet and back. Mostly plastic, bottles, tackle, and many deflated party balloons. Loved the freedom of walking alone, fresh air, flora blooming in the brush, and the quiet. A communion with nature, my own rehab.

Most employees during summer months were high school or college students. I was known as "The Old Guy" or "The Crazy Old Guy" when I suggested they change the bucket water before mopping the rest rooms each morning.

After a while I never spoke much to anyone and kept to myself. Things seemed to work better that way. I was there to regain my physical strength, not make friends with kids young enough to be my children At lunch I would sit in my car with sandwich and water. Radio, "Music of Your Life" on a local AM station. "And now the No. 1 tune of 1955, Perez Prado's "Cherry Pink and Apple Blossom White." As the trumpet slid down and then up before the melody, my eyes closed, and my thoughts would drift back to Rockaway in the summer of '55. My mother handing me an egg salad sandwich wrapped in wax paper and a cheese glass of grape Kool Aid. Then thinking that I sit here twenty miles to the East, looking at the same ocean, listening to same tune, trying to preserve that Mambo spirit in my heart.

My summer job was just what the doctor ordered.

My last day would be September 13, a Thursday. On Friday I was scheduled to start rehearsals for the Arthur Miller play "All My Sons." We were supposed to open on October 25 at The Hampton Theatre Co. out in Quogue. This job was actually a good physical warm-up for my role.

On the morning of Tuesday, September 11, with my helper Robert next to me in the cab of our pick-up, we set out to pick the beach. While driving along the high tide line where much of the debris lines up, Don Imus's voice came crackling through our walkie talkie. Imus said a plane had crashed into the World Trade Center. My first thoughts were this is a terrible radio prank, but soon learned differently.

A feeling came over me similar to the morning I was wheeled onto an elevator to go up to the operating room. Cleanly scrubbed, things were out of my hands now. Suddenly I prayed that morning at the Beach, as I did on the elevator at St. Francis Hospital.

My heart ached for the victims. For their families. For all of us. And I knew that morning what my young co-workers were to find: that we are helpless at times, and at times we are the helpers.

LYNN EDELSON

Lynn Edelson is a special educator and family trainer in the New York State Early Intervention Program. She is the mother of two grown sons—a writer and a musician—and says she's fairly certain neither one will ever buy her a beach house. In 2016 she was selected for the New York City cast of the "Listen To Your Mother" show, and for the past five years, she's studied memoir at The Writing Institute at Sarah Lawrence College. Though often accused of writing poetry, Lynn is currently at work on a collection of short stories.

DOG DAYS

Lynn Edelson

I'm at the circus asking the man behind the hotdog counter for a job. He looks at me and smiles. "How old are you, kid?"

What I want to say is, How old do I have to be?

"Fourteen," I answer reluctantly. Because after all, I am still my mother's daughter. Honor and integrity. No child can possibly live up to those words, but they are her guide posts as she parents us.

"That is not honorable," she says quietly. Not, go to your room. Not, you're a liar. But, where is your integrity?

He looks at me again. "Fourteen, huh? You got working papers?"

"I left them home," I lie. Because I am also my father's child. He grew up on the streets of Brooklyn when his family didn't have enough money to buy food for his six brothers and sisters. Honor and integrity were luxuries he could not afford.

"Well I can't pay you a lot," the hotdog guy says. "But come back tomorrow with your papers and we'll see."

9

I tell my mother I'm going to be selling hot dogs at the circus, for the 10 a.m. show. If she signs the form for the working papers today, I can pick them up tomorrow.

"You're too young," she says, shaking her head.

"I'm going," I tell her.

"Ask your father," she says hoping he'll say no.

My father says yes. He likes that I'm scrappy like him.

I work one shift and then two. I imitate the guy who yells to the crowds. Get your hot dogs here, get your hot dogs. And people line up and hand me money and smile at my moxie. I laugh and eat hot dogs for breakfast and know I'm exactly where I'm supposed to be.

"Hey kid," the hotdog guy says, as he hands me four dollars. "I can't pay you for the second shift today."

I'm not sure what to do. "But you said I could work," I say.

"Yeah, but this is how these things work out sometimes," he says as he hands me an extra fifty cents. "Think of it as your training day."

Training day? I sold more hotdogs than he did.

"Come back tomorrow and we'll see how it goes."

We both know I'll be back.

STEVEN LEWIS

Steven Lewis, Literary Ombudsman for 650, is a columnist at *Talking Writing*, and a member of the Sarah Lawrence College Writing Institute faculty. A longtime freelancer, his work has been published in *The New York Times*, *The Washington Post*, *Christian Science Monitor*, the *Los Angeles Times*, *Ploughshares*, *Spirituality & Health* and others. His novels include *Take This* and *Loving Violet*, both from Codhill Press, and Finishing Line Press published Steve's poetry chapbook, *If I Die Before You Wake*. His backlist includes *Zen and the Art of Fatherhood*, *The ABCs of Real Family Values*, *The Complete Guide for the Anxious Groom*, and *Fear and Loathing of Boca Raton (a Hippie's Guide to the New Sixties)*. He divides his time between his writing space in New Paltz, New York and Hatteras Island, North Carolina

HOT AND SWEATY

Steven Lewis

Summer mornings during high school, my best friend Richard and I would drive to work in New Hyde Park where my father owned a small school supply warehouse next to the tracks. There we'd unload hot, rusted freight cars filled with heavy cartons of paper, then stack the cartons in the dark corners of the hot warehouse, pick and pack detailed orders of school supplies, and at the end of the day, our white t-shirts soaked in sweat and blackened with soot and rust, load trucks headed for schools all over Nassau County. It was hard work.

Because we were teenagers—and no doubt because my father was the cigar smoking boss—Richard and I would occasionally steal away from our jobs by hiding in private "caves" we had constructed while stacking the floor-to-ceiling cartons of paper in the warehouse.

During those stolen minutes, against type, we didn't smoke cigarettes, didn't drink beer, didn't leer at Playboys. Mostly we just leaned back and talked about nothing. Or didn't talk. It didn't matter. In that cave of cartons, it was just me and my pal, a boy much like me who had no expectations of who I was or who I might become in the unformed future. In that cave I didn't have to pretend that I was someone other than the lazy, empty-headed, confused, horny, pimply-faced boy that I was.

After work, I'd go home, shower, guzzle dinner like I was filling up at the Mobil station, and drive off to my night job: moonlighting as a boyfriend to a girl named Judy. Far more emotionally and intellectually challenging but no less physical, our evenings usually led to hot and sweaty making out in parking lots and cul-de-sacs all over town.

Then, after racing to get her home before curfew, I'd clock out. But I wouldn't go home. I would drive around that dark, nothing-happening town, sometimes for hours ... looking for Richard.

He had the same night job. Different girlfriend.

Empty-headed boys that we were, we never once arranged a time or place to meet after our dates. Instead, we drove through the cookie cutter suburban neighborhoods, up and down the service roads on either side of the L.I.E., radios blaring in synchronized distant stereo, until one of us would finally spot the other ... and we'd pull off the road ... one getting out of his car, sliding into the other, yanking the passenger door shut.

Although it is hard to imagine now, when talk is at the heart of all my intimate relationships, I can't remember ever having had a serious conversation back then with Richard—about anything.

We'd sit shoulder to shoulder, often for hours, staring out through the windshield into the darkness, finger drumming or air guitar-ing along with whoever Murray the K was playing on WINS.

And later, back home, all alone in my narrow bed with only my confusion as company, the sun soon coming up on another work day in the hot warehouse, I sometimes wondered if I loved Richard more than Judy. All things considered, it was a lot easier being with him than with her. Having a girlfriend was hard work, a confounding job for this profoundly befuddled boy. Beyond the breathless pleasures of baring our sweet and sweaty bodies to each other, I had to talk. I had to figure out what made her happy, what made her sad, what made her angry.

With Richard, there was no need to talk, there were no expectations, no sexual or romantic tensions, nothing to get right. Nothing to go wrong. We'd just find each other in the warehouse cave or some hours later on some dark suburban lane, lean back and, for a few unfettered, uncomplicated, unemployed minutes, escape all that hot and sweaty summer labor.

KAREN DUKESS

Karen Dukess has been a tour guide in the former Soviet Union, a newspaper reporter at the *St. Petersburg Times* in Florida, and the founding features editor of *The Moscow Times* in Russia. She has written book reviews for *USAToday* and blogged about raising teen-aged boys at *TheBlunderYears.com* and the *Huffington Post.* Her narrative non-fiction has appeared in *Intima* (Columbia University) and her short story, *Fancy Hat,* appeared in the 2017 issue of the *Westchester Review*. She is a speechwriter at UN Development Programme and is a member of the Terzo Piano writer's group. She lives in Pelham, New York.

THE GIRL IN THE BACK ROOM

Karen Dukess

On summer mornings at Motif Designs, women in tennis skirts flipped through fat books of Marimekko wallpaper. With tilted heads and pursed lips, they contemplated the implications of choosing the cheerful orange poppies instead of the sophisticated green ferns. They scrutinized nearly identical paint chips and asked if Venetian blinds would make the right statement for the living room.

I was seventeen and had interest in none of it. Working in the back office, I was bored—in a 1980, pre-iPhone, pre-texting friends from the bathroom, pre-Candy Crush kind of way. Just me and a pile of invoices and purchase orders, an adding machine that chewed up rolls of paper and a slow, noisy fax machine. The job's saving grace was that it was mindless enough for daydreaming. As I typed up estimates, my mind drifted to memories of the nights before, when I'd snuck into Manor Park with my boyfriend, and thoughts of the days to come, when I would finally leave home for college. I didn't know precisely what I wanted from the future, but I knew it would involve writing, adventure and romance, would take place nowhere near suburban Larchmont, New York, and would never require the services of an interior decorator.

One morning, I peeked out from the back office to see the store owner consulting with a man with jet-black hair and dark sunglasses. It was our local celebrity, Eyewitness News anchor Ernie Anastos. With shades remaining on, Anastos joined his wife in discussing new décor for their home, a stone house with turrets that stood at the end of a winding driveway behind a tall iron gate. I knew the house well; as a girl, whenever we'd drive by, I'd strain my neck to look at the castle, hoping to see the princess who lived there.

Now, I was less impressed. Watching the couple finger fabric swatches, I whispered to the twenty-something office manager, "If I ever end up anything like them, someone had better just shoot me."

You know where this is going, right?

As I type, I'm in my house, about six miles from the site of Motif Designs, where there is now a bank. My husband is at work, reporting on the economy for cable television. One son is down the road in high school, the other across the country in college. I am back at my laptop after taking a short break to have flat Roman shades, selected with the help of a decorator, installed in my bedroom.

Is the ambitious girl in the back room at Motif Designs disappointed? Probably.

I'm pretty sure she would be pleased to know she would get romance and adventure: A newspaper job in a swampy Florida

18

town, years working in Russia, and marriage to the adventurous guy who was willing to go along for the ride. But she would be aghast to learn that by her mid-thirties, she would move to the suburbs, where she would raise two children and work a Mommy-track job everyone would say she was lucky to have.

For much of my adult life, I had that girl on my shoulder – sometimes pushing me forward, occasionally holding me back with her naive beliefs that learning the art of compromise is not a good thing, that a twenty-five-year marriage can't possibly be romantic and that you can't have flat Roman shades and be a writer.

But as I neared fifty, I had an epiphany: I'm wiser than a seventeen-year-old girl, and old enough to tell her to shut up. And when I did just that, the best of her spirit came through. So now, when I sit down to work on the novel I am finally writing and determined to finish, I can hear her girlish voice, brash and hopeful, urging me on.

JOHN GREDLER

John Gredler, poet and memoirist, is a frequent contributor to 650 who's been writing in notebooks and journals for most of his adult life. He honed his craft at the Writing Institute at Sarah Lawrence College, Bella Villa Writers, 125, and the Terzo Piano Workshops. A recipient of the 2014 Gurfein Fellowship from The Writing Institute at Sarah Lawrence College, John's work has been published in *Atticus Review, Fictionique, Narratively, Dan's Papers, Westchester Review,* and *Talking Writing.* John lives and writes in Tuckahoe, New York.

WILLIE

John Gredler

That summer my mother would come into my room every morning and leave the Help Wanted section of the newspaper on my bed. Or on me, still lying in bed. She had circled possible jobs in red marker.

I dragged myself to the Youth Employment Service and applied for the first job that sounded okay: painting the Olympic size swimming pool at Badger Sports Club.

I showed up at eight one morning to meet Willie, an old black guy wearing overalls and a pork pie hat, a cigar stub stuck in the corner of his mouth. He looked me up and down, stopping at my long hair. Then took off his sun glasses and looked me over again. He spat without taking the cigar out of his mouth.

'We got to get them leaves out.' Willie said handing me a rake.

Empty, the pool looked immense, a blue rectangular void.

The leaves in the deep end were wet and slimy. I slipped and fell on my ass at one point. Willie just shook his head and turned away. After we raked the leaves, out we mopped the entire pool. Then he told me to mop it again.

When we finished I asked, 'Are we ready to paint now?'

Willie snorted, "First we got to get the pitch outta them seams" spitting some nicotine- stained saliva too close to my foot. He squatted on an overturned five gallon can, lined up a chisel and hit it with his hammer. The tar shattered like black glass.

Then Willie handed me a bucket with a hammer and chisel, work gloves, and goggles inside. He watched me line up the chisel and hit the seam. It shattered, spraying me with obsidian shards.

"Not so hard. Make sure you keep those goggles on."

For the next few days we inched along a few feet apart, the pitch exploding under the blows of our hammers. As the day wore on, I would strip down to my tee shirt. By the end of that first week, a rash broke out on my arms and neck. The skin turned brown and began to peel off from the bits of pitch hitting my exposed skin.

"If you keep that up you'll be black as me." Willie grinned.

"Why didn't you tell me?"

"You seen me, didn't you?" he said holding up his arms, long sleeves tucked into his gloves, his shirt buttoned all the way to his neck.

As the spring days grew warmer, the tar became a soft sticky mass. We'd cut into it along the edges and pry out gummy wedges of black taffy until we cleared it all out.

"Tomorrow we pour the pitch," Willie said, lighting his cigar stub.

He told me I'd be carrying the molten tar from the parking lot to the pool. We would use metal watering cans with the tops taken off to fill the seams. When he was finished pouring one, he expected me there with another full can. It was a hot day, the metal cans full of tar heavy and scorching even with the thick gloves I wore. It went like that all day.

The next morning, we took long poles with rollers attached and started to apply the thick blue paint. In the afternoon, we were in full sun. As we rolled out the paint, thin membranes like cobwebs peeled off the rollers and rose up in the heat, gossamer webs of pale blue floating just above our heads.

I was captivated, wanting to see how high they would rise before falling into themselves in twisted ropes, or disappearing into the sun.

When we finished. we were both spent, Willie fell asleep under a big oak tree. I sat on the edge of the shallow end gazing out at the pool, a glimmering oblong of turquoise which, as I stared at in the sunlight, seemed to levitate out of the ground.

JENNIFER RAWLINGS

Jennifer Rawlings is an award winning writer and performer whom you may have seen on Comedy Central, CMT, PBS, FOX, VH-1, A&E, CNN, HLN, CURRENT, *The Joy Behar Show*, or her two recent TEDx talks. Named in 2014 as one of the "21 Change makers of the 21st Century" by *Women's E News*, she's performed in over 350 military shows including in Iraq and Afghanistan. Jennifer's directorial debut—Forgotten Voices: Women in Bosnia received critical acclaim, has screened at film festivals worldwide, and is part of the curriculum at several universities. She's written books, for television and film, and for numerous publications including *The New York Times* and *Reader's Digest*. In addition to cooking, cleaning, and driving in circles, Jennifer—the mother of five children—is currently finishing a new book and touring her solo show, *I Only Smoke in War Zones.*

A KANSAS TAN

Jennifer Rawlings

Salina, Kansas. Sixteen years old. Dusk was settling in just as my dad and I settle on the front porch. My dad in his lawn chair—Pabst Blue Ribbon, pipe full of tobacco—me on the porch swing with pink can of Tab.

The mosquitoes are chewing my Coppertoned legs, but I don't care, I have an agenda:

"Dad, can I have some money to buy tickets for the Summer Jam concert?"

This was going to be the most important concert of my life. Reo Speedwagon, Styx, John Cougar...before the Mellencamp." EVERYONE was going, I had to be there too.

Puff, puff, on the pipe . . . tamp down with the corner of a matchbook. My dad's answer, slow as a smoke ring: "It's time you earn your own spending money—get a job for the summer."

"DAD! I don't have time for a job. I have THINGS to do. Why do you hate me?" I sobbed. I ran up the stairs to my bedroom; dropped the needle on Supertramp "Breakfast in America."

I wasn't lazy, I didn't have time to work.

I had my driver's license, though. I needed to drive with my friends to the mall . . . to the liquor store. We loved the liquor store on State Street. It was called State Street Liquor. The owner had the posture of a question mark and despite his horn-rimmed glasses, he wasn't that sharp. He carded me every time because the sign said "we card everyone." And every time this sixteen-year-old walked out with some hooch.

We drove to the banks of the Smokey Hill River, drank beer, and inhaled the secondhand smokes we had swiped from our older siblings.

I had a boyfriend, Richard Johnson . . . Dick Johnson. Making out in the back seat of Dick's rust colored Chevy Chevelle with vinyl interior was an important summer pastime.

I didn't have time for a job.

But I was going to have to get a job . . . if I wanted to go to Summer Jam. My parents were digging in. My mom wanted me to work at Dillon's grocery store. My dad wanted me to work at his law office. But I was still hanging onto my summer plans of getting drunk with my friends and getting a tan.

Then it hit me . . .

Four years earlier we put a swimming pool in our backyard. In case you don't know, Kansas is nothing like California. A backyard pool is a terrible idea. It's snowing, raining, lightning, or a tornado is coming 320 days a year.

So my summer job . . . I'm going to give swimming lessons in my backyard.

I hadn't taken life guarding, nor given a lesson on any subject, but I was on the swim team.

Half a dozen students signed up.

Eight-year-old Wade Chung was one of my students. His family had just moved to Kansas from Korea. On a sunny Thursday, Wade took a double swimming lesson because there was a tornado the day before. As she was writing me the check, Mrs. Chung asked, "Do you know anyone who could teach Wade French?"

"Well, yes I do; I can teach Wade French."

I taught Wade everything I knew: We counted to ten. I taught him the word for cat, dog, months of the year . . . not in order. I taught Wade six days of the week.

My summer job was MUY BIEN . . . I had money for Summer Jam!

The big day arrived. 180 miles to Kansas City.

Afternoon: Triumph, Loverboy,

Evening: John Cougar, and then the band we had waited for our entire teenage lives . . .

REO SPEEDWAGON about to take the stage . . . when the music stops, lightning crashes, thunder rolls, the sky turns from blue to black, the air grows still, tornado sirens blare, heavy rain falls—and the PA instructs us to follow the signs to nearest tornado shelter.

Where we sit for the REST OF THE NIGHT.

"This is merde," I say.

That means shit in French.

Wade knows that word, too.

SARAH BRACEY WHITE

Sarah Bracey White is a writer, teacher, and arts consultant. A graduate of Morgan State University and the University of Maryland, she's a former Inaugural Fellow at the Purchase College Writers Center. Published work includes *Primary Lessons: A Memoir The Wanderlust: A South Carolina Folk Tale,* and *Feelings Brought to Surface,* a poetry collection. Her memoir piece, *Freedom Summer,* was included in the anthologies *Children of the Dream,* and *Dreaming in Color, Living in Black and White.* Her essays appear in *Aunties: 35 Writers Celebrate Their Other Mothers, Gardening on a Deeper Level,* and *Heartscapes: True Stories of Remembered Loves.* Her essays have appeared in *The New York Times, The Baltimore Afro American Newspaper, the Scarsdale Inquirer,* and *the Journal News.* She and her husband live in Ossining, New York.

CAMP COOK

Sarah Bracey White

In 1963, days after my graduation from a segregated South Carolina high school, I boarded a train for Ely, Vermont, where, even though I knew little about cooking, I was to be the head cook's assistant at an exclusive girls' camp nestled on the shores of Lake Fairlee. I dreamed of learning to swim in the beautiful lake pictured in the camp's brochure. Upon arrival, however, Camp Beenadeewin's owner told us that the kitchen help was not allowed to go near Lake Fairlee. We also were told not to associate with the white campers, and to address each one as "Miss" during all encounters in the dining hall. Up north, it seemed, segregation was a matter of class and skin color.

I was incensed and wanted to bolt; but, I had no way to get home, and no home to return to. My mother had died a few months earlier and I'd had no contact with my absentee father for years. Beenadeewin was to have been my interim home until I entered

Morgan State College that fall. The camp's offer of room, board, a round-trip train ticket, and $300, in exchange for two months' labor, no longer seemed fair; but, I accepted my fate.

Mrs. Lee, the head cook, six other teen-aged girls and I quickly settled into the routine of preparing and serving home-cooked meals for 150 people, three times a day, six-and-a-half-days a week. It was cold and dark each morning as I made my way through the pine-scented forest to the kitchen where I stirred huge vats of Maypo, loaded slices of white bread onto an industrial-sized toaster, then buttered and pressed each slice into a plate of cinnamon sugar. Under Mrs. Lee's tutelage, I learned to make, and enjoy, delicacies like sugar cookies, clover-leaf dinner rolls, and smooth, brown gravy for pot roasts.

Despite my anger about the restrictions at camp, I was shamelessly curious about the campers. Never before had I been in such close proximity to so many white people my age. From my side of the kitchen counter, it grew easier day-by-day to eavesdrop on their conversations as they grew used to our brown presence and we became about as insignificant as the pine trees.

I soon learned that white skin brought no solace from money problems, didn't ensure smooth boy/girl relationships, or prevent sadness and heartache. They had the same problems I had! I also learned that having two parents at home didn't always make a happy family.

Every Sunday afternoon, the resident handyman took the seven of us sightseeing in the camp's old, woody station wagon.

I marveled at the beauty of the Vermont countryside, and the quaintness of its villages. I surmised from the stares that our little group always drew that no other colored people had ever lived in, or visited, the state of Vermont. An overwhelming sense of being different, and unwelcome, permeated my entire experience. I vowed that once I left Vermont, I would never return.

The last Sunday afternoon before camp ended, instead of joining the weekly tour, I made a pilgrimage through the pine forests to the forbidden Lake Fairlee. As I looked out over the vast, mirror-like expanse, I grew angry. What right did white people have to bar me from something God made? Since they thought my skin would contaminate their lake, I decided to do something that really would. I stepped into the water, squatted, and peed.

SALLY HIGGINSON

Sally Higginson is a columnist for *The Chicago Tribune*, providing a humorous twist on the chaos of life for nearly a decade. For seven years, Sally co-hosted a nationally syndicated radio show called *Walking on Air with Betsy and Sal*, which led to *The Betsy and Sal Show*, broadcast on Chicago's WGN radio network. A Dartmouth College graduate, Sally worked as Photo Editor at *Woman's Day* and *Outside* magazines, then earned a Masters in Education from Northwestern University and taught high school English. In addition to *The Chicago Tribune*, Sally's work has appeared in AOL's *Patch* and the *Chicago Sun-Times*. Sally has emceed several charity events and performed at Moth events.

SCREEN DOORS

Sally Higginson

One summer during college, I decided that working on a sheep farm in Vermont made sense. Nothing in my suburban life had pointed me in this direction, and I confess I wasn't really a huge fan of animals, but I was determined. I wanted to get strong doing manual labor.

With the unbridled energy of the young and the foolish, I learned to hook bales of hay, and stack them in a loft. I learned about intensive grazing, moving fences, and sheep in intricate patterns across the fields. I grew to love fresh eggs enough that I was willing to suffer the ammonia-rich stench of the chicken coop. I didn't sheer the sheep, but I stood in the stifling July heat of the barn, scooping up freshly shorn wool as it fell from each ewe. I fed animals, and buried animals. Every day, I got strong.

At night, I walked the hundred yards away from the family's yellow farmhouse to my own tiny cottage. Inside, it was spare. A single bulb hung from the ceiling, and near the bed where I slept sat a radio, connecting me to the world.

The first two weeks, I fell asleep instantly. The third week, however, I started listening to music, letting Vermont Public Radio's classical music help me drift off. One night, an announcer interrupted the program. "This is a warning," the deep voice said. "Two convicts have escaped from a North Carolina prison, and are believed to be heading north through this region. They are armed and considered extremely dangerous."

I sat up. I looked around. And then I tiptoed over to where the front door should be, but wasn't. In its place hung a screen door with a hook-and-eye latch. Lifting the hook, I fitted it into the little round eye, trying to secure myself from the two armed and extremely dangerous convicts. Then I got back into bed, pulled up the covers, and waited to be murdered.

In the morning, when I woke up alive, I walked to the yellow house and called home. "Mom," I said, my back to the farm family. "Could you please send me my Raggedy Ann?" I like to think there wasn't a quiver in my voice, or shame in my throat. In truth, there were both. During the week it took for my doll to arrive, NPR failed to report on the whereabouts of the convicts. Each night, clutching only fear and fatigue, I willed my eyes shut. Spoiler alert: I did not die.

Since I lived, I learned a few things. I learned that I was strong enough to work on a farm. I also learned it takes strength to acknowledge danger exists beyond my control. There will always be escaped convicts lurking just beyond the screen door. That I believed a latch-hook, or a Raggedy Ann, could keep me safe was both foolhardy and necessary. It's instinctual to seek protection, but naive to believe in invulnerability. Faith, even in a rag doll, has its place in the world.

All these years later, I live in the threshold of screen doors. The untamed winds from outside pass in, and the filtered air from inside escapes out. The boundaries blur, which is the point of the screen, while the framework remains in place, which is the point of the door. It's the closest thing I have to understanding the need for control, and the recognition that the longer I live, the less of it I have. Being strong enough to accept that truth is hard for me. That summer on the farm taught me no matter how strong my muscles, nor how pure my faith, the unpredictability of life does not yield. There will forever be things over which I'm powerless.

BLAIR GLASER

Blair Glaser is primarily an executive leadership coach and organizational development consultant. She has written on leadership, empowerment, and intimacy for a variety of magazines and web publications including *The Huffington Post* and *The Good Men Project*. She co-leads an annual writing workshop for women, *Women Writing to Change the World*, at the Omega Institute in Rhinebeck, New York. Blair is working on a memoir about living in an ashram in her twenties.

THE SWAMI'S ASSISTANT

Blair Glaser

Invisibility beckoned.

The Catskills ashram I'd been intermittently visiting since January was accepting a few summer applications for people to do seva, or "selfless service" -- a.k.a. work -- in exchange for room and board. Ever since I stepped into the ashram's cavernous kitchen with the sacred chants streaming through the speakers and engaged in the blissful task of chopping carrots for 3,000, I knew I wanted to stay for a while.

Trying to be an actress in New York City at twenty-three was, well, trying. I'd been at it for a few years, squeezing acting classes and auditions in between my two waitressing jobs, one uptown, one down. I was sick of the grime and the noise and the striving and the rejection. But waking up to the pre-dawn sky and the sweet smell of incense, meditating, and losing myself in menial tasks, connected me to a deep, quiet hum: the music of my being. I wanted to immerse myself in it.

I booked an interview and got a ride upstate to the ashram.

On the wooded path from the dining hall to the main building, my daydream about spending my days wearing a shmata on my head, doing dishes and quietly chanting the name of God, was interrupted by a small cluster of people gathered on a footbridge. A salt-and-pepper, short-haired, red-robed swami sat on the ground, clutching her ankle. She was hurt. Help was on the way. The only thing I could do was close my eyes and offer a prayer that she would heal quickly. I continued on to my interview. They grilled me and told me to come back in two weeks.

Two weeks seemed like an eternity, but when I arrived back in the seva office, the smiles on the formerly stern faces of the directors seemed promising. In fact, I was told, an "interesting" opportunity opened up. The assistant to an injured swami left to deal with a family emergency. Would I be interested in replacing her? I immediately accepted, although the position was nothing like the chopping and cleaning I'd imagined. It wasn't until I met Swami S. that I remembered her from the bridge, and that I'd said a prayer for her healing at a time when I never would've imagined actually being a part of it. Wow, I thought, in this place, my prayers are literally answered.

Well, sort of. Instead of hiding in the anonymous cave of the kitchen, I was out and about, meeting the Swami's colleagues, students and admirers. Plus, Swami S. was cranky. Fiery and in her mid-forties, she was not used to being infirm, or dependent. I discovered there was no home emergency; the prior assistant left because things "didn't work out." Sometimes, Swami S. had to snap me out of my spaciness. Other times, I got lost in morning meditation and arrived late with her breakfast, her chilly irritability greeting me at the door. And then there was my New York Jewish tendency to analyze her.

In response to her edginess, I would say things like, "Maybe you're just sad about the things you can't do." Once, I responded to her complaining by saying, "Aw. You'll feel better once the cast comes off."

She hissed, "No. I'll feel better when you get out from inside my head and focus on your job."

It's the kind of comment that packs a punch—and sends well-meaning assistants packing. But it was also true. Later that day, I went for a walk to shake off the sting and reflect on doing a better job. The wind rustled the luscious leaves, chuckling with me at the idea of coming to the ashram to cocoon myself in bliss. Instead, I ended up facing myself, and learning about real, live intimacy with another, flawed human being.

One to whom I eventually became a very good assistant.

.

DAVID MASELLO

David Masello moved to New York more than thirty years ago from Evanston, Illinois, and he has made his living as a writer and editor ever since. He began his career as a nonfiction book editor at Simon and Schuster, then went on to hold senior editorial positions at many magazines, including *Travel & Leisure, Art and Antiques,* and *Town and Country*, where he was features editor. He's currently executive editor of *Milieu*, a magazine about design and architecture. He's a widely published essayist and poet, with pieces appearing in the *New York Times, Salon, Best American Essays,* and numerous literary and art magazines. His plays have been produced and performed by the Manhattan Repertory Theatre, Jewish Women's Theatre of Los Angeles, Big Apple Theatre Festival, and Fresh Fruit Festival. He is the author of two books about art and architecture.

WHERE I'D LEFT OFF

David Masello

There came a point when I was seventeen where my fifty-nine-year-old father needed me to help him find work. I'd been hired to paint a room in a warehouse on Chicago's northside and I was to be alone all day in the windowless space, with a transistor radio and gallon can of white paint. I propped open the door to the outside, but remained wary since it faced a glass-bejeweled alleyway.

I liked painting houses and rooms, just as I liked mowing lawns and shoveling walks in my neighborhood. For these tasks, I drew straight lines—in grass, on walls, along sidewalks—until I'd transformed the surface into something else. I knew where to begin and when I'd reached an endpoint.

The warehouse was owned by a friend's father, who manufactured restaurant equipment. My friend's father and mother hired me every summer to paint the outside of their house, which remained so white and clean year to year that during my work, whenever I stopped for a break, I had trouble finding where I'd left off.

The factory/warehouse task was different. As I rolled on the paint, the space brightened with each application, and I, too, as a mist of white speckled my arms and hair. I heard the crunch of glass from the alleyway—and in walked my father, dressed in suit-and-tie, his attire as a wholesale liquor salesman. Workdays for him consisted of driving to bars, hotels, nightclubs, restaurants, bowling alleys throughout Chicago to see clients who ordered their liquor through him.

But he'd lost that job—and my mother—though gaining a new love, a woman for whom he'd soon leave my mother. The woman worked at my father's company and through a misguided scheme, she'd assigned my father an inordinate number of commissions. They were both fired.

"How did you find me?" I asked my father.

"I was meeting with your boss," he said, "seeing if there might be something here for me. I sold booze to restaurants. I can certainly sell pizza trays. But he said he didn't have anything for me."

I was too young to know the significance of my father's plight, a man then my age now, jobless, on the cusp of a new life with a different woman. He was leaving, too, a spacious home in a leafy North Shore suburb for a ground-floor apartment in Chicago in its last Italian neighborhood.

My father was an affectionate man, forced to shake my hand that day, given my paint-spattered overalls. "Maybe on the drive back with him, you could ask again if he might have something for me," my father said.

A month later, my father and mother drove me to Ann Arbor, where I was entering college, my first time away from home. My father had yet to find work, but even for the 250-mile drive, he was dressed up. When we arrived at my dorm, my father got out of the dinosaur-scaled Chrysler, hugged me, and wept. He got back in behind the wheel. My mother got out of the passenger side, hugged and kissed me, and wept.

They were saying goodbye to me and to their marriage.

I was so inexperienced I didn't leave my dorm room for an entire day. That next afternoon, my mother called to tell me my father had moved out. He was old-fashioned that way, waiting for the last of the children to leave home before he did.

He found work as some kind of messenger, delivering tickets. Many years later, after he'd moved to Florida with his woman and I was in New York working as a magazine editor, I mailed him weekly shipments of review books I'd been sent by publishers. He sold them to a bookstore and kept the money, making friends with the owner.

As his woman friend told me, "You've given your father something do, a new friend, and a place to go."

ANNA PARET

Anna Geraldine Paret first came to New York as an investment banker transferred from London. She's lived in America for over twenty years—in Palo Alto, California, Washington, DC, and New York City. Anna and her husband currently live in Larchmont, New York; their oldest daughter attends university in England, and their youngest in Washington, DC. A former docent at Jasper Ridge Biological Preserve at Stanford University, Anna is presently a naturalist at Sheldrake Environmental Center in Larchmont. Her work has appeared in *Orbis #173*, *Inscape*, where she received the Editors Choice award for the poem, *What is the Grass?* and *Ghost Town Literary Magazine*. She is a 2016 Scott Meyer Award short story finalist.

HOMEMADE JAM

Anna Paret

Shwoom ... shwoom ... blasting wind from speeding traffic picked up the cardboard sign—Homemade Jam—tossed it over the hawthorn hedge and into the field of ripening barley. That summer, I worked part-time at a pick-your-own market garden, picking fruit to be sold at the farm stand. I was allowed to take home as many punnets as I wanted. I think.

My best friend Judith said let's make jam, I know how. And ... and ... we can collect jumble—secondhand clothing, used books. We can make calico skirts, elastic at the waist, draw Chinese characters on them. We can sell stuff at Milton Keynes flea market. Every other Thursday. Or once anyway.

We reduced the soft fruit with sugar, added lemon juice for the pectin. We boiled empty jam jars to sanitize them, and filled them to the brim. We covered the lids with gingham mop caps, left over swatches from school summer-uniform dresses.

We arranged the jars in a pyramid on our allocated stall. We hung the cotton skirts from the awning, in front of the previously worn dressing gowns, cardigans, office shirts yellowed under the arm. We unfolded two camping stools in readiness for a long, busy day.

Judith opened a rubbish bag of gently used shoes; strapped sandals, high heels, brogues in need of polish. "Don't unpack them," said a man in a cloth cap. "I'll take the lot. Two quid."

I hefted a box onto the trestle table. A man with a full, gray beard watched me open it. "Books? Three quid for the box," he growled. The market hadn't even opened yet.

At half past nine, the shoppers began to drift in. By ten thirty, they filled the walkway like herded sheep. A woman picked up a pot of jam, turned it over, and put it back. A teenaged girl fingered a skirt. Her mother shook her head. "Too short," she said.

Three stalls down, the shoes were selling for 50p a pair. Across the aisle, the books went for 60p each, some a pound. We sold a jar of raspberry jam. By the end of the day—books and shoes wholesale; one jar of jam—we had made £5.30. We were rich. In jam.

"Let's stop on the way home," Judith said. "Sell it roadside." Great idea.

To make a sign, I tore a panel from the box of unsold nighties, and borrowed a marker pen from the sweet old lady who ran the stall next door and who, it seemed, had sold an inordinately large number of hand knitted tea cozies. Bed jackets. "Thanks for buying the jam," I said to her.

Then Judith and I crammed our goods into her mother's Hillman Imp, and drove out of Milton Keynes. "How about here?" Judith said as she bumped the car onto the grassy verge and stopped.

The road was straight. An approaching driver would have a clear view of us for a good 500 yards. Behind the parked car, I set up a camping stool, draping one of the more attractive secondhand dresses by way of a tablecloth, weighed down by jars of jam. Judith retrieved a large stone from under the hedge, and wedged the cardboard sign—Homemade Jam—against a small sapling.

Cars sped by … shwoom … shwoom. Laughing, her calico skirt flapping with every gust of wind, Judith plucked the spinning sign from the air, and returned it. Peeled it from the side of the hedge, and returned it. Chased it down the road, and returned it. Squeezed under the hawthorns, crawled through the barley, retrieved it … and tossed it into the back of the Hillman Imp.

Years later, I came across a jar of gingham-topped strawberry jam on the top shelf of my parents' larder. It was a little runny. But so good on toast.

KATHY CURTO

Kathy Curto teaches at the Writing Institute at Sarah Lawrence College, Montclair State University, and across the metropolitan area serving writers of all ages. Her work has been published in the anthology, *Listen to Your Mother: What She Said Then, What We're Saying Now,* in publications including *Barrelhouse, Drift, Talking Writing, Junk, The Inquisitive Eater, The Asbury Park Press, Italian Americana, VIA-Voices in Italian Americana* and *Lumina.* In 2006 she was awarded the Kathryn Gurfein Writing Fellowship at Sarah Lawrence College and also served as a 2015-16 Engaged Teaching Fellow at Montclair State. Kathy lives in Cold Spring, New York with her husband and their four children.

CLOSING TIME

Kathy Curto

It's the summer after graduation. Until my father finds somebody to replace Chip, the guy who got busted for stealing from the cash box, I'm working at the car wash every day except Sunday. My parents opened the car wash a few months ago on a small piece of property behind what used to be Fred's Texaco but what's now Holiday Service Center. So now the family business is called Holiday Service Center and Car Wash. Which is hilarious and pathetic at the same time.

Holiday is the opposite of what I'm on when I come here.

I get in at eight o'clock in the morning and leave at half past five. I let the last car go through at five o'clock because by the time I count my cash box and record the day's numbers, it's about a quarter after five, which leaves me the last fifteen minutes to open the safe, put the money in, double check the master water valve, and triple check the breakers before locking up.

But yesterday, a lady pulled up in an old, rattling Buick at ten after five. I was counting the singles when I looked up and she rolled down her window.

"Sorry, we're closed," I yelled through the opening between the glass door and little office space that is my grotto when we are slow, and nobody wants shiny cars. It's where I read and wonder what heaven looks like.

She yelled back.

"Please, sugar, my girl needs a cleaning real bad."

I shoved the stack of singles in my pocket and walked toward her and her Buick. The hood was speckled with residue of rust and bird shit. Her stubby, dry fingers flew across the dusty, maroon dashboard. Coffee-stained letters and what looked to be unopened bills fell to the floor of the passenger's side.

I leaned into her open window to say, "I started closing out my cash box already, ma'am—sorry." but then I smelled a weird combination of salami and rubbing alcohol. My eyes moved from her fingers to her hair, which was black and greasy, but some was gone. Portions of her scalp showed.

"Yeah, I guess she kinda does," I said, and turned away to look at the main operating panel that held the buttons for all the washes and waxes and shine options.

Then I looked at the grimy hood of her Buick, the car she calls her girl.

Then I looked at the hairless spots on her head.

"Please, sugar," she pleaded, "I got a five here somewhere."

She turned away and opened the glove compartment. Now it was ketchup packets and what looked like an old black and white photograph of a man in a soldier's uniform that fell to the floor, landing on top of the letters and bills.

"Why don't you go ahead and take your foot off the brake and put it in neutral, ma'am. I got this one today."

Free washes don't happen every day here. My father says it's company policy to save the free washes for good customers, people who are regulars. I never saw this woman before. Not even once. Definitely not a regular.

She's very much irregular.

And that's the reality that knocked me down. Her irregularity and all that went with it—the smell of salami, the bird shit, the old ketchup packets, her girl: the Buick—all of this, suddenly, mattered.

I thought, What if?

I imagined her sitting in a fancy, swiveling beauty parlor chair, her legs crossed, a cup of tea in one hand and a slick magazine in the other, her hair being styled in a shiny high beehive.

I looked one more time at the soldier boy on the floor.

Then I pushed hard on the blue button labeled "The Works at Holiday" and watched her and her girl fade into the last wash of the day.

EDWARD McCANN

650 founder and editor **Edward McCann** is a writer whose features and essays have been published in national magazines and literary journals such as *Better Homes & Gardens, Country Living, Good Housekeeping, Milieu, the Sun,* the *Irish Echo* and others. An award-winning television writer/producer and longtime contributing editor at *Country Living,* Ed is a member of New York City based Artists Without Walls and Irish American Writers & Artists. He's recently completed a memoir about the search for his missing nephew, and his essay, "Pregnant Again," was selected for the anthology, *Listen To Your Mother,* published by Penguin Books in April, 2015. He lives and writes in New York's Hudson River Valley.

WORKING PAPERS

Edward McCann

I was twelve years old when my parents sold our house in Queens and moved with my older brother and me to Deltona, a retirement community in central Florida where elderly men putted golf balls into cups on their lawns and occasional posses of elderly women could be seen pedaling giant tricycles through the streets. Everything was alien and new, including the thick green lawn surrounding our house. Neither my older brother nor I had ever touched a lawn mower before, and as first-year Floridians, we argued about whose turn it was, as if cutting the grass were actually a privilege.

An elderly neighbor soon offered me $10 to cut her lawn. Ten bucks was more than my weekly allowance, and I could earn it in just a couple of hours. Grass grows fast and thick in Florida, and my new gig put cash in my pockets for the first time in my life, enabling me to buy model car kits, a ten-gallon aquarium filled with tropical fish and a bubbling treasure chest, and the first store-bought gifts I ever gave my mother. Business expanded when my neighbor introduced me to her widowed friend a few streets over who needed her lawn mowed, and within a month I'd taken on a third elderly customer even farther away from home. With my inner entrepreneur awakened at thirteen, I purchased a new mower that I towed behind my bicycle as I pedaled along the winding streets of our sleepy development, steering with one hand while maintaining my grip on the mower's handle with the other.

I quickly learned that summer in central Florida is scorching hot and miserable. Tromping back and forth behind a push mower while trickling perspiration burned my eyes and soaked my shorts soon got old, and my interest in cutting other people's grass faded even as my tan—and my voice—deepened. Dad said I was building character, but I thought maybe I already had enough character, and I was sure I'd had enough with the lawn mowing. I wanted a "real" job. Unfortunately, I had to wait until I was fourteen, when the state would issue my underage working papers.

Dad signed my application and on my fourteenth birthday I returned it to Mr. McGinnis, the school guidance counselor. In exchange, I received a blue, wallet-sized work permit—my entrée into semi-adulthood and a passport to my first real summer job. I was eager to stop working outside in that oppressive heat and humidity, to leave behind those overgrown lawns and the trickling perspiration that burned my eyes and soaked my shorts. I applied for jobs around town, calculated bike routes, and imagined my air-conditioned self working behind a cash register alongside my new "friends from work."

I was thrilled to be hired at T.G.&Y., the discount department store anchor of a busy, sparkling new shopping center with palm trees in its parking lot. I was shown how to punch in and out for my shift, and was taken on a tour of the aisles, the stockroom, and the layaway cages. I used my employee discount to buy a new work shirt and tie to wear beneath my dark blue smock. I felt proud to see my name professionally printed on a plastic placard pinned to the polyester, and Mom took my photo wearing it when she and dad dropped me off for my first shift — the day I learned, too late, how I'd actually be spending my summer.

I was given a box cutter and escorted through the stockroom onto a loading dock flanked by a pair of giant Dumpsters. The blacktop below was littered with bulging trash bags and dozens of cardboard cartons in every size, with more arriving every hour — boxes that had contained the "merch" that was now displayed on the shelves. My new, on-the-books, minimum-wage summer job was trash jockey, breaking down and flattening boxes and filling the Dumpsters, while standing beneath the relentless Florida sun, on blacktop, in a polyester shirt, tie, and smock, as trickling perspiration burned my eyes and soaked my shorts.

SUMMER JOBS

ACKNOWLEDGMENTS

In addition to the contributors to this volume, we thank City Winery's Founder & CEO Michael Dorf for the invitation to produce a live event at The Loft at City Winery. We're also grateful for the support of City Winery's National Production Director, Marc Colletti and Talent Buyers Hannah Gold and Len Chenfeld.

CityWinery.com

We thank Nancy Manocherian's the cell, which supported 650 at its inception. A twenty-first century salon in the heart of New York City, their mission is to support the arts and incubate new works, and the cell made its beautiful performance space available to 650 as we were finding our way. The cell: To mine the mind, pierce the heart, and awaken the soul.

TheCellTheatre.org

Artists Without Walls was created to inspire, uplift, and unite people and communities of diverse cultures through the pursuit of artistic achievement, and has supported and encouraged 650 from its beginnings. Artists Without Walls: No Limits. No Walls. No Boundaries.

ArtistsWithoutWalls.com

READ650.COM

INFO @READ650.COM
FACEBOOK.COM/READ650

SUMMER JOBS

Made in the USA
Columbia, SC
22 May 2018